FOR THIS AND OTHER CRUELTIES

KUHL HOUSE POETS

Lisa Wells and Joshua Marie Wilkinson, series editors

Mark Levine, advisory editor

FOR THIS AND OTHER CRUELTIES

YOUNA KWAK

University of Iowa Press, Iowa City

University of Iowa Press, Iowa City 52242

uipress.uiowa.edu
Printed in the United States of America

Cover design by Susan Zucker
Text design and typesetting by Ashley Muehlbauer

Printed on acid-free paper

Library of Congress Cataloging-in-Publication Data

Names: Kwak, Youna, author
Title: For This and Other Cruelties
Description: Iowa City: University of Iowa Press, 2025. | Series: Kuhl House Poets
Identifiers: LCCN 2025002979 (print) | LCCN 2025002980 (ebook) |
ISBN 9781685970284 paperback | ISBN 9781685970291 ebook
Subjects: LCGFT: Poetry
Classification: LCC PS3611.W345 F67 (print) | LCC PS3611.W345 (ebook) |
DDC 811/.6—dc23/eng/20250407
LC record available at https://lccn.loc.gov/2025002979
LC ebook record available at https://lccn.loc.gov/2025002980

CONTENTS

DEATH OF THE MOTHER

No mamas. No murderers.

—GRETA GARBO

I am preparing to write a book
about the death of the mother. To write
such a book requires a mother
who does something remarkable or real
in an apprehensible way, or

a secretive mother
whose tics and tacs construct
an almanac, aphonic archive of
the inner life, rustling
with hushed facts, or

a mother mammoth
and serene, gliding across your path,
so the shadows of her limbs scratch
out upon your face some blood
narrative. The book

about the death of the mother cannot repose
on interest as mothers are not
interesting. In her guise as mother
she slips soundlessly into the garden
of disinterest at dusk, where

even wishful squinting calls forth only
drab husks. Mother is made
of failed forms of intrigue, except insofar as
her artful mothering casts diamond lights or
nettled shadows on those she has

mothered. Loosed from her mother-
bindings, she may be a creature as strange
and alive in the world as any other. Then, to be
alive will be her business. But mother
mothers, mothering is her business. Mother—

sole citizen of a world beyond
boring, too hunched and
formless to be caught in the flashlight
sweep of someone's surveillance. Suspected
of nothing. Nothing to see

here. She did this and that, then came
I-obliteration. The book of the death
of the mother desires
to retrieve what is last, exultant task, to reap
the reward of the overlooked, who back

slowly away into the drift of your
history, arms full of discarded objects. Only
as mother can she be
subject. The book about the death
of she-who-is-known-as-mother

is a different book entirely. Though such
a person may exist, having never known her, I am
unfit to write the book about her.
In the moment of my birth
my mother was born as mother and

so will remain to me after her death,
after my own. Or lacking all these
to write the book about the death
of the mother you simply need
a mother, who is dead.

DODO MOTHER

Yeti, mermaid, unicorn, fairy, siren, medusa, mother
before mothering, conjured from word of mouth

or inherited memory with no proof of actual existence as any
creature who can't be known, only believed,

a deity or disappeared, phantasmagoric being a matter
of faith, mistress of fabricated fabula, the dodo

supposed, whose droll-faced walk was once without pareil, then
swiftly snuffed by a grimy thumb upon the page. Gather all

your credulity, your taking the others' word for it. You alone,
arriving late to shore after the feast of slaughter, can have

no recollection of your mother-before but for seeing her maiden's
name memorialized in the museums of your nothingness, the truth

of her past imminent with the immutability of her present
nonexistence. Was-once creature, already myth, too dupe

to defend her birthright to flight—sluggard wallowing
in the unflinch of fearlessness, in spite of her false mien

of tenderness, in spite of looking so possibly
delicious, the dodo looked far into her future extinction

within the world of your disappearance, where she lived
in the world without you, your great-grandparents babies, who

grew up, had babies, were grandparents, who grew up,
had babies, were aunts, uncles, and your not-yet

mother, all children alive in the world
of your nonexistence, beyond the reach

of your imagination. Imagine your mother
in the world where you are not, absent before the fact

of your future, imagine her crowing,
how she smacked her lips against the nothing

of you, her freedom from you a garland of fragrant blossom
without thorn, neither hibiscus nor roses but

viburnum and jasmine, shedding fragrant leaves,
just as she was sturdy yet endangered, yet unburdened by

predators, sparkling with the light of brilliance early
extinguished, a creature whose only enemy could be human.

BAD MOTHERING FABLE

Once long ago in a large resplendent city in
the populous East, a young mother was caught

shoplifting a carton of milk with her six-month-old baby
gurgling cluelessly in the cart. The clerk who caught her

scolded her specially for stealing in front of her child but
stopped short of calling the police. The chastened

mother wept and promised she'd do better. Wasn't she
also thrilled? Didn't she give a sly wink as she

almost got away with it? Didn't she say
I'm sorry I'm so sorry silently

cackling? Didn't it feel so juicy and busted, bad
mothering in the moment of being

mother? Years later in a large rundown complex in
the populous West, the self-safe mother home

alone with two children, in need of an ironing board
to iron her husband's shirts, put the baby

in the crib, tells the toddler *stay inside* and gone
in a flash. All the way home she sweats

and struggles, the ironing board banging, bawling
deep bruised beats: *left my babies alone*

now my babies are dead. Soon the horror
mantra turns from dirge to bright song: *left my babies alone*

now my babies are deaaaaaaad. Wouldn't mother love
to be a bad mother? How badly must you mother

to be ousted from the garden? Isn't bad mothering
a hot shove of relief? As Lacan once kind of said, if

a woman who thinks she must mother's deluded,
a mother who thinks she must mother is mad. Mind, it's no

Shangri-La to hoe row after row of infinitely hungry
mouths, doing all the planting, harvesting, weeding, year

after year, fall after spring, come drought or flood, wolf or demon,
every yewling open mouth needing rescue, one

gardener, no staff, no scaffold, no airbag or oasis, no
Plan B, no mutual aid, no life raft, buoy, or maintenance

crew, no parachute or safety vest, no getaway car, just
mother.

SOMETIMES MOTHER

Guess who appeared in the living
room on the night of parent-teacher
meetings wearing underwear, pantyhose,
blouse, but no skirt, crowing *Let's go!*

Guess what she did with the fat
envelope of cash from Elder Brother
supposed to go toward fixing
the washing machine. Guess what she was doing

home "sick" on Wednesday afternoon
in the empty house, guess what happened, that time
she was careless, guess how little
she remembers, how the memory

scarcely troubles. What reasons for not
knowing present their sly, upturned faces? Won't
tell, won't remember, all lies, wasn't
asked—guess who's compelled

to endanger her children to satisfy some
material or psychic need, acting rashly, feeling
sorry, expressing contrition, resentment, regret or
else just punished, anyway still yoked

to the mother-script even if not
feeling sorry at all, some joyful
smear of not-sorry feelings, defying
classification, inadmissible sear

whose sullen opacity jolts, scorched
jab of pleasure each time you gingerly
poke, aching to evade the bars of the mother-
cage that no amount of badness can bend.

ANYONE'S MOTHER

In a faraway city across an ocean and a bay, after
two hundred and sixty days of not having seen her

children, a friend's mother dies before he can visit. No
possibility of a funeral. Though no season seems apt

for the death of the mother, this perpetual shattering, daily
detonation of dozens of dying mothers, certainly

takes the cake. Anyone with a dead mother, whether once
amiable or disastrous, recalling what their mother

once wore or ate or what she never always used to say,
their voice catches slightly in the throat, snap

of a wrecked wing, one heartbeat before the crash. In
a faraway city a mother shoved to the pavement near

a busy intersection is repeatedly kicked in the head by
a passerby shouting racial epithets and *go back*

to where you came from. Most impressive
are the placid doormen seen on surveillance

appearing to observe the beatdown through
the open door of the building and then in observance

of her prone and shaking body on the sidewalk, shut
that door. *That could have been my mother*. Every mother

beat down on the sidewalk anyone's mother. Every mother
kicked in the head *that could have been my mother*. Becoming

or not becoming mother not germane, both choices belong
to the world of mothers, concession to being or not

being mother, neither yielding the neutral point of the world
without mothers. Having or not having a child are but two

sides of a coin of expired currency. Not being mother won't
divest you of having a mother, for there is no human alive

who has no mother whether mother is known, unknown, present,
abstract, concrete, visible, divined, biologic, accidental

or metonymic for the emotional fabric of the world. Our
belly buttons prove it. To be motherless not possible

in a world where every mother could be
your mother. The only meaningful choice not having or not

having a child but to consent, as if life pressed its quick into
this close silver, to the death of the mother.

MAMA KILLJOY

God forbid the father even the barest
speck of joy. When he has busied making

meanness last, going back and back as
far as the horizon of the core rotten world

ruled by the mean daddy of her worse daddy plus
the soon-to-be-mean daddy she married,

during all those years when I was trying
to get thin, look pretty, become someone

a boy would want to pet, she was already bones
and arrows at the surface deflecting and in the depths only

death—at best!—the only definite. Death
is the good news, living's the connivance. In her

hoary heart she loves too hot to let in any happy or love's
invariably the wrong question. The right one

is mama squelched, given no issue. We'd love
to kill the father too, for keeping

her under thumb and foot, her labor
looped to turn the sad days bad, the bad

days sadder, this too a task of mothering, as
our love was a thick sole's squash upon

her febrile lights, her love a smoldering stitch
dousing out our every needy bursting into

flame, her every calm *fine* to the how-are-yous
a ruse as she laid patiently in wait to intercept

the imminent arrival, the pain of the world a parcel
she intended to deliver us by hand.

OUROBOROS MOTHER

trains me to seek constant approval so I constantly
disapprove of mother and she constantly
disapproves of me so that our mutual
disapproval defangs the specter of disapproval.

To feel weak and damaged, not to feel at home
in the world, to feel out of place, unseen, unsafe
everywhere are defaults that mother considers
proof of superstrength for despite the failure to

belong, you are here. Mother always came last
as if it were her destiny to be forgotten, but even
destiny is rememberingly narrative. If story
giving value to mother's life is anathema, not

to tell mother's story is unethical, if story is tidy
melodrama then failure of story may be
corpse. If story of mother is unjust then failure of story
true life, if only as Mother she's permitted to enter

story, the no-story now provides
resolute shapelessness, before settling into
the familiar likeness of phantom, before it can be
harnessed, corralled and smushed into the story

of the death of the mother, which despite all storms
will hold steady to story with you as
protagonist, a deep cake of color dissolved
in water so that something very like

Mother might emerge, divested of metaphor
or destiny, an entry
into peculiarity where you do not want to be
protagonist, you too want merely to live.

MOTHEROLOGY

Once upon
a long time ago
a friend wants
a ride to
a faraway place where
he plans to meet
his other friends but
when you arrive
the friends are
nowhere
to be seen and you are
reluctant to leave
him there alone
in the middle
of nowhere whereupon
he says: *but*
the moment you leave
my adventure begins.

That day you
too became
a mother.

MOTHERING

Taking over

me, don't know how to be cool

about it, trying to be

cool isn't it pitiful I'm not

cool at all I smell

bad so worried all

day want so badly to do it

right instead all day just cry

and cry on the airplane cry when

she's screaming cry

in the grocery but mothering's

still my new best skill my only

skill it's what I do

most now am best at no more

work no more writing only crisis and

the only center that holds having to stay

alive for the sake of she's

overtaken me maybe will

choke to death maybe

drown if I look away one

minute now she's four she says

very pink, pink brown, light brown, very brown now

she's six says mommy what does rape mean now

she's eight already hips are curving my hands

in my pockets perpetually making

fists now she's ten getting ready I can

tell by her side look she's sharpening

the long knives looking in

the mirror preparing to

use them meanwhile

I'm stabbing at another

skill trying to be more

than this though can think of nothing

else but I also have a brain every day

so fogged with the nothingness of

everythingness every day veers

away can't be cleared out every day

devastated by some ordinary sadness

of my mother's so ordinary but

her suffering has to pierce

someone inevitably and that must be

me and my suffering has to pierce

someone inevitably and that must be

how we found

each other here dead-

locked into arrangement as

mothering and

mothered.

MURDERMOTHERING

Being born means being pushed, pulled, or cut
out of a womb, meaning, mother becomes in the moment

she says *Out*. Becoming mother foretells the art
of injury, meaning, withholding your care

is no glancing blow, always fatal parry, never
provisional, always definitive, colonial in

forcefulness, even petty harms symptomatic, can't
do without you, somebody's feelings can't

be helped, the intoxicating condition of being
mother, a life in your hands, can you love just

a little and mother, can you be loved just a little
and mother, the mothers of mothers are murdered

ceaselessly at a distance each time without
story, each time mother dies again a little, watching

one by one the faraway lights extinguish, feeling
future in their presence, the mirage they are and

were not attached to obscure survival, all
this time I felt it was shame that gripped

and held me in check but it was only
love, a tiny love, just a little bit of love,

to be a little-loving father only mis-
demeanor, only mother's little bit

of loving's felonious, little
enough to kill.

DEATH OF THE MOTHER

for D. K.

In a suburban American city three thousand miles away from
her adult daughter, an aging mother suffers a "mini-stroke." Only

many hours after the collapse, the rush to urgent care, the spiriting away
into the shrouded No-Information-Kingdom called

Hospital, does she receive this suspect and obscene though
medically appropriate diagnosis. Whatever

can be qualified by the prefix "mini"—golf, skirt, van—comes
to life with brutal, bulbous, cartoon villainy, sneering at mother

as she lays in imagined disarray on the hospital cot where she
was tossed, a launderer's bag filled with bones, deep

in the sepulcher of the ER, as the father paces the waiting
room for six hours having been told to *wait here* with

no further instructions. He waits. Hours later, a head pops
out: *waiting for a neurologist.* Next a whole lot

of nothing. What to do at a distance
of more than three thousand miles? S., whom

motherlessness has made wise, says *call
the hospital, say: I need to talk to my mother.*

Mother is indeed *waiting for the neurologist, no idea
when he'll get here,* she feels *fine,* but *mad*

at the rude nurse calling me honey. Fine but pissed *I'm*
not your honey. Still, after waiting all night

to see the exhausted, overbooked neurologist who's been
shuttling between two hospitals since the first days

of confinement, she and the nurse make up, no hard feelings, *you*
should be nicer to an old lady who's sick, I hear you

honey I hear you before she's released and allowed to return
home with her aging husband, thoroughly depleted

after twenty-four hours of unrelenting anxiety, although mother
remains perky, alert and annoyed. The only person who

earns her praise is the attending physician *just call me Dr. P.*, eternal
concession of the immigrant with a talent for customer service, who

we gather, from mother's cagey description, is young and
good-looking, Dr. P. who says *if you were my mother I'd be*

overjoyed, you had the exact kind of stroke I'd want my mother to have!
After the long moment it takes to deconstruct

the optimism of this perplexing statement the mini-stroke will be
referred to as *the kind Dr. P. wants his mother to have.* Two days

later, it happens again. ER, lobby, waiting, phone, nurse, CAT
scan, MRI, ultrasound, neurologist. Who's asking for an eternity, god

forbid, just a little more time, a dieter's meager pie crust of time, a tick
tock of a minute or two before she goes, so that we might be

in the room together for a breath after the death of the mother,
let mother die, long live mother. I am the one

who will remember best, who will say your name last, who
will accompany you into the second death, the last time I pronounce

your name, I will be loosened into the flat field of solitude's char, free
to wander, let loose into the wilderness of visionary care, pressing

forward with my own survival, emptied at last of regret, as if
needing only rain barrels lushly full of desert rain, the fire pit

with its fragrant cedar, so much joy, Mother, that no one else
but we might enter.

MOTHERSLANG OR THE VERNACULAR OF PIGEONS

Who can say who's foreign within
the closed principality of likeness comprised

of mother and me, sole
citizens of a country of two, blood

bound yet each indecipherably Other in
language, where we both adhere to

furious idiolects, like when my mother texts
why are you so mad I didn't mean

to make you mad and I text I'm not
mad at all there's no need

to get upset and she texts back who's upset
I'm not upset why are you

upset and I text back I'm not
upset you're upset. Now that she's fragile

and her legs no longer work, mother
says *I'm stupid, I'm weak*, or *I'm*

afraid, not *I'm beautiful, I'm*
strong, I am your mother. Our relation now therefore built

on disbelief, whatever I say she disbelieves, whatever
she says I refuse to hear or won't listen or the words'

insistent worming lost in transit in the ear canals, via
phone, FaceTime, Zoom, as if twirling intemperate

tentacles down a blocked passage. She is a muted stampede
of wants and I am the grass trampled under cloven hoofs or

vice versa. Whatever she wants to hear is
unpronounceable. Whatever I want to say is drowned out

by the lawnmowers of the world, mowing
to their foregone conclusions. I am not listening

to my mother as she is telling me now how no one
listens, describing her state of not-being-

listened-to in the manner of immigrant mothers with insolent
American daughters but also just a mother

not-listened-to-in-the-world whose footfall
so discreet so as to leave no print, whose call

so muffled so as to fail to arouse reaction, before
it's bluffed out completely, dowsed in an avalanche of thick,

white snow, her condition of not-being-listened-to inciting
the condition of not-being-addressed, says mother

aloud, as I say *hmm*, also trying to enter upstream like
any other mother-loving salmon hustling through white

muscle. *Mother* a word, not metaphor, semantic, not malignant,
lexical, not fatal, still the pidgin flaps through, broken-winged

in accordance with no discernible form or genre. If her vocation's
to survive, then no book about the death of the mother

and nothing specifically interesting to tell. Until
she steps across the book's threshold, gathering the folds

of her clattering skirts, where all her secret
singularities are scattered, shiny as empty spoons.

PREULOGY

We all know *Mother* means
I was born from your body but I too
guaranteed your living.

In the mothering reign where
you are always alive, alone and evenly
breathing, a place

of exile where you remain
a figure leaning lazy on a rock,
black spot of ink bored into sand,

whoever you were when shone
bright as the aberrant luminescence blazing
death's yearly visitation

of the ocean, what it meant
for me to wear your face
surely different from what it meant

to you to see me borrow it,
I say this now before
there will be

no you to say it to
during the long winter of unforgiving,
brittle summer of not

forgetting, mother, we are
as water and soil, peas
of a wither, when I was

a child and you inconsolable,
I thought my care remade me
a mother but now having grasped the barb

of mothering and been remade
a child and you my mother, we
two swept back together

into childhoods bereft
of children where you and I were
thick as sleeves

stuffed with plunder
pillaged from the unloving world, our
loving saying you as mutely

as the stone that determines
the direction of the current, fast
waters where aloneness

mimics feeling safe
from harm, fished for me
everything and anything you wanted

ever even the sharpened teeth of sadness
acute with wicked appetite, Mother
to whom I am bound by likeness,

who will one day
eventually die, our being
here together is a meeting of like-

minding, being mothers we are bound
to obey the heroic strain not-
withstanding desire to walk

lightly over crusted snow leaving
barest impress, to have seen you
cry cursed me with a talent for confession, epic

in mythic detachment, for the means
to embrace the swaddled curve
that will one day be your body

I forgive you now knowing
you will leave this task undone
when you are gone, having said so little

it will fall upon me then to say *old slights*
can never be repaid
and that's a fact

she made her choice and stuck to it
to sail blindly forth on trust
seconded by internal rage

enraged by the mere sight of snot on children's faces
she wiped our noses so often and so roughly
just thinking of it now makes my nostrils sting

the cracking sound she made when chewing gum
was a sound I tried to imitate for years
clacking tongue against palate

like her I am not
the forgiving kind

LIKENESS

Living is not an original business.

—YIYUN LI

CAT LOVE

A monk appears before God at the end of a long and pious life, expecting to be commended for having given up all of his earthly goods to devote himself fully to serving God, and is astonished when he is instead reprimanded for having given too much attention to his cat. My cat? he repeats, stupidly, uncomprehending. That poor, pathetic, downtrodden animal whose creaturely life he had undertaken to save, with no more reward than its mute companionship and loyalty? Yes, your cat, says God, unmoved by the humility of this account: You love your cat too much. And thus the monk is barred from heaven.

But what would it look like, to love just a little?

THE YOU YOU DO OR DON'T RESEMBLE

I am more like Simone de Beauvoir than I am like my dentist Simone Choi. Simone Choi prefers American bistros when she goes out to eat and she doesn't drink. She's a Mets fan, which I am trying to be also but can't muster the interest. We have nothing to talk about although since my mouth is usually agape in her presence and her fingers in it, the silence feels like part of our collusion.

I am more like Hélène Cixous than I am like Simone Choi even though the hygienist pretends to mistake my dentist and me for sisters. He's joking but he has just cause. Beyond the racial profiling, we do look alike. Also, we are the same height, and we have the same build. We were born in the same year and in the same city and we know the same words to the same songs. We heard Michael Jackson's "Thriller" on the radio at roughly the same time and were bullied by basically the same kind of white boy during recess at suburban public elementary schools that sound more than a little alike.

I am more like Beauvoir than I am like Simone Choi, I am more like Cixous, I am more like Barthes, more like Emily Dickinson, more like Sylvia Plath. What does Simone Choi think about when she's intently lasering the plaque from the inner ridge of my lower gums? Is she thinking about the Subway Series? Is she thinking about our sisterly resemblance? Or about her real sister, of whom she is less than fond, who lives in Fort Lauderdale and is both difficult to visit and difficult to host, what with her insistence on particular brands of particular foods and territorial attitudes about sharing a single bathroom between four adults and three children?

I am more like Proust than like Simone Choi, who also watched the Towers fall in real time from a street corner in Lower Manhattan, who also became eligible to vote during Clinton/Bush Senior. *It's so terrifying what might happen,* a sophomore said to me on the eve of the election as we studied together for a European Women's History exam on the Quad. As it turns out, I didn't have a clue what terrifying could mean, and neither did she.

SUBURBAN FABLE

Once upon a long time ago the family moves to a green and desolate cul-de-sac in the white suburbs where every afternoon after school, a gaggle of mothers assembles to take a leisurely walk around the block, and in the seven years you live in that house as your mother's daughter, they never once ask your mother to join them. In this way, you understand your mother is not like other mothers. So, too, does your mother enjoin you to be *not like the other girls*, and by *other girls*, she means the white girls who are loud and slutty and disrespectful. Why you would aspire to be like a slovenly white girl is a question beyond your mother's understanding, just as she cannot comprehend why you insist on attending the homecoming game (*when you hate football*) or plead to be allowed to go to the dance with a boorish boy who gets bad grades (*because he asked me*). Your mother's and your alikenesses are entangled with aspirations, which are nothing alike. Stripped of aspiration, likeness is but a banal descriptor. When they humiliate the daughter, she stays up all night, restless with bewilderment, wondering: Why is she so unlike the others, what makes her so different, what makes her so wrong? But when they try to humiliate the mother, she wonders: What makes these people so stupid, ignorant, and selfish? And the mother pities them in that brief moment before their faces recede into the sludgy backlit scree of all that is disagreeable and inconsequential, having nothing to do with her.

I LIKE I DON'T LIKE

I want to know whether I am like my mother. I have to ask the question while she's here. Once dead, she will drift into difference, my aliveness cause for an irreparable rift, an epistemological obstacle heading me briskly off from the meeting point of our alikeness. As long as she is alive, we are both survivors, and this commonality superglues us together. I survive being her daughter, and she survives being my mother, and together we survive the hostile glances and reprobation of everyone around who finds our ways of being mothered and mothering incomprehensible, pointless, and pig-headed

Was she strict asks my therapist

Why so ungrateful asks my mother's friend

even though we exercised no choice in the matter, even though we were born in the same moment as mother and mothered, bridled to this configuration from the moment of first exhale on earth, the newborn as an autonomous human body, concurrent with the first inhale of she who was newborn as mother.

▪▪▪

My first friends were the children of my mother's friends, Mexican, Ecuadorian, Venezuelan, Pakistani, Irish, Greek, Lebanese, Korean mothers speaking the universal language of *cállate* and *siéntate*, our harbor against angry fathers, who came home exhausted from terrible jobs, struck us, threw things, and yelled. The fathers' rage was externalized into a crashing opus of hands and fists, while the mothers' rage burned bright interior bonfires, fires that lit our way, by whose lights we might glimpse what we would later become, far away from our mothers and fathers. The mothers did not strike us, nor did they defend us, their pity tempered by the memory of worse fathers.

▪▪▪

We were tall, short, skinny, chubby, brown, black-haired, wily, smart, lazy, disobedient, docile, harmless, malicious children, all alike. Our lives were so alike, our fathers so alike, their anger alike, the way their differently accented voices flared into sudden rage alike, our mothers' insolvency alike, the helplessly competent way they did everything that needed to be done while failing to earn a penny to ease the financial burdens of our pissed-off dads, alike. When one of us got lice, we all got lice. The mothers argued about whose child was the cause, but without conviction. Each knew it was the other's child, and each was so certain she was right, there was really no point in arguing.

▪ ▪ ▪

Fractious families, aloof white classmates, hostile clerks at drugstores where our mothers sent us with a quarter to *please just go away,* sidewalks not made for walking anywhere, the rec room where the chairs were always soiled, the playground swings where we clustered to make our secret, arrogant, definitive plans, here where friendships were arranged marriages, their convenience and suitability undeniable. None of us belonged in America's genial, white-hot world. Our alikeness forced open the doors of *like,* barreled us straight into a cloister of sticky, jealous, turbulent love, where we wrestled ourselves into existence.

▪ ▪ ▪

There was no difference then, between my mother and me, between my mother and her friends, between me and my mother's friends, between my mother and my friends, between my friends and me—I could have sworn my mother and I were the same person, our silhouettes crushed together on the illustrated timeline of the Cycle of Life, the figure representing the Age of Childhood superimposed over the Age of Adulthood, creating the palimpsest of Us, a two-headed, four-legged, four-armed creature glumly stuck in an Age of Child-Adult-hood, speaking out of two mouths without discerning anymore which one was accusing and which one denying, which one attacking and which defending, which confessing and which exulting at the confession: *I knew it.*

▪▪▪

The story of belonging is also this: wanting to be like the others, in the hopes that by knowing them, you could also know yourself, but without having to do any extra work, because what a dizzying pleasure, knowing them, and what a mind-numbing slog, to know yourself. And if asserting a choice was what made you different from the others, we made the choice to be unconcerned about choosing. We had none of us chosen our mothers, our cramped apartments, our bullies or fathers, our stupid haircuts, what we ate, what we wore, and yet here we were, doggedly alive, alike as kin, *I like I don't like,* our likeness pressing obdurately forward toward burnished human form.

BETTER MIRROR MOTHER

Mothers endeavor to give their daughters the childhoods they dreamt
of having. But mothers' dreams arise from the memory
of specific deprivations or unfulfilled desires, which belong
to them exclusively, so that their efforts to compensate for
the deficiencies of their own childhoods, however
impassioned, can only engender new, unexpected
deprivations for daughters who dream differently.

Daughters endeavor to give their mothers the deaths
the daughters dream of. But even in death, desires
are singular, specific, nontransferable, not alike, so
that the deaths daughters dream for their mothers are
at best, only sort of like what mothers desire.
This is the bathroom of my dreams says
my mother to her reflection applying

cold cream in the second mirror over his-and-hers sinks
adjacent to a cream-tiled sunken bathtub abutting
a matching stand-alone shower and toilet in the master
bathroom of the house to which she has moved post-
immigration plus decades of peripatetic existence lived
in rented houses on American army bases, and I learn (*I like
I don't like* but yes, her body, my body, not the same)—

there are bathrooms in my mother's dreams.

AS IF

I will make myself at home in the as if.
I will make a home there, faithfully, totally,
in the as if.

—ROLAND BARTHES

THE NATURE OF TOGETHERNESS WILL SCARCELY REVEAL ITS FACE

In the possessive case   *my students*   as if
mine. How are they

mine   in what way do they belong
to me and   how do they possess

me, who is also   theirs. Their teacher who will someday
        be a collection of boots, bone, rag if

everything goes my way   if I am lucky
trilling luck   as we must be

to survive   then my students
        will tend to me.

Right now I'm in charge.   One student cries
in my office saying *I believed you*

when you said you believed
    in me   Did I say this? I thought only

        how I must be better, for my students,
how I must not yield.

My white colleague says   there are so many Chinese
students   they are difficult to understand.

She says this easily as if   misunderstanding poured
        indifferently down   like rain.

The president says   we are careless with our water
and this is the cause   of our fiery misfortunes.

The firefighters   who are not idealists, say
          fire can't be fought with water.   It's lack of rain

that is to blame.   Lack of rain,

          lack of rain
          lack of rain
          lack of rain
          drought
          drought
          lack of rain—

The president's always angry and accusing
          whatever he says I want to stand

between the words   and my students
not to be their hero

but out of shame. To muffle   the shriek
          of the creature we shoved   into their room,

locking the door behind us. Reading
with my students I hear the words   come

out of my mouth   when the students ask
          and the words are   *bête noire.*

When the students ask
          What is *bête*?   What is *noire*?   They are

assembled. Some of them are
scapegoats   and pet peeves. I think so hard before I speak

then have spoken
          and the words have begun

their long journey out
into the trampled forest of feeling   names, dates, pronouns

hopes, remonstrances, nagging doubts and dreams   and will
          not tamp down into the dirt. One student cries

because I have humiliated her by
accident.   Writing this down, do I further the harm?

Would that the poem be
          a balm   a smoky offering at the altar

of the gods who lately   deserted
          my students   and me. Under the eye

of the gods of deprivation
          here we huddle together and are

equal.   Another student is
hungry but for everything.   Her appetites will not yield.

And why should they?
          Would that I could be

     their cornucopia
     their cup runneth over
     the feed bag infinitely replenished

would that I could alter   the world
to abrogate   their deprivations.

I am but a humble servant though
whom do I serve   I cannot now discern it. Discernment

also a job to which I am
tasked   being the teacher

of my students. They   restless as
a horde of hydra seeking deep succor and relief. One

wish   *to deprive them*
        no further.

No gods apt   for prayers
        which might   relieve their burden.

They are difficult to understand because
creaturely by nature   I am limited

        in understanding. Leaving me
they enact my death   and if I wished

them to write me a eulogy it would say

        profoundness of gratitude
        profoundness of grief
        profoundness of encounter

what comes to mind when my students
        enter rustling   gathering in to root   leaving my door

ajar.

COMMON FORM

If you should split all your infinitives, evidently
the device would lose its peculiar efficacy:
the locution would become mere common form.

—SOCIETY FOR PURE ENGLISH
TRACT NO. XXXVI (1931)

But I would prefer to not get drawn   into
especially the way
you allude to the past
the precious few hours I have today for
the inner resources
for the sake of my emotional
myself what needs my attention
a moment of crisis, very
fraught
spread too thin I've made every effort
we're scheduled to
as far as I know
not to cause you harm in order to
carefully choose my actions
no time is either good or bad but
Mondays, Thursdays, soften certain truths
respond at length in writing
interpreted as defensive and
threatening
every effort during our long relation
make time to really
talk any time
do see how that priority may have
let this process unfold can I
make it work

have to be able to let go to believe
the few reserves too
fragile as we all
nor any attempt at moving toward
the healing
I've been able
to lately think of nothing else
since I was surprised to hear you attribute certain
feelings
how poorly you might judge I
communicated a dozen drafts
did not in the end
whatever the reason for whatever reason
just because in these twenty-five years
did nothing to convey
to you what I felt
contradictory but unsurprising
no idea to what extent

SOME INTERESTING THINGS WERE SAID

when we were together, many

interesting things spoken

aloud in my presence or

whispered as if none might come

to fruition— “none” the word

of the cynic

disbelieving of the path

out of the forest some interesting things

were said

when our coming together had lost its fine momentum

each trying to explain

to the other

the difficulty of surviving

in the room where we were lately

together each trying

to explain

what seemed obvious and true what

had happened in the room

where we each

thought separate

thoughts that met

through separate bodies

that could have no purchase

except through touch its

magnificent order I would not have wanted

a different life but only

to be different-

ly within this life with a temperament

to better endure its petty confusions if I chose

a different body it would not be

a white body but a body

with no hidden recess for shame if I had

a second life I would not

want a white life but one in which

I would not begrudge myself

a chance at splendor

some interesting things

were said

when our coming together had lost its purpose

each trying to explain

what the outcome would be

in the presence of shame and all its coordinates

winding dazed ways down the canals of no light

where sustenance goes and turns

to undigested forms

of what we swallowed

that refused to go down— "refusal"

the word of the optimist

not that I wanted to live in a white body

but did not say as much

or what I said was not enough

when we were friends

unwilling and

together

as if attentive—   “as if”

the pledge of the cynic

who must survive on the hypothesis

that nothing will change

I was there in the room in the night when

everyone tensed and grew still—   “everyone”

the word of the optimist

stillness of the pattern of light

by which you could see more clearly

among the others

by virtue of being so wrong and so small

together so small

in allure and in persuasion

LOOKING

after Leo Steinberg

What gesture receives?   the hand splayed   over
      blue cloth crumpled   how hands form
a gesture of blessing   the hand splayed   look
  carefully to the fingerwork forget your confusion   how
hands form   a gesture of blessing   obedient space
      look to the fingerwork   forget your confusion
what cannot be pictured   obedient space   the light
  of two suns   what cannot be pictured   ten thousand
      or what is innumerable   the light of two suns
the shoulder's tend toward   ten thousand or what is
  innumerable   if we survive   the shoulder's tend toward
      what would keep me from looking   will we
  survive   why stop looking   in the center of
the dish   I don't think anything   could stop me
    looking   why stop looking   as I have eyes
      I don't think anything   could stop me from
looking   blue cloth crumples   at the center of the
    image   as I have eyes   as a dog lays
      its jaw on your thigh   not the posture but
the interaction   in the center of   the dish
      a lemon   waxed   not the posture
  but the interaction   the body rises   will you
believe   the body falling   caught my attention
      will you believe   human life
over blue cloth crumpled   if we survive   why stop
    looking   what would keep me from looking
ten thousand   or what is innumerable   tend.

READING FRANK O'HARA ON THE METROLINK

What more can be said
        of the every day that is neither monumental

lie nor monument   weekly I take
        the train past Fontana Rialto Rancho

Upland harrowing   rarely tranquil   I am
        though grateful as rarely to be

myself and not some other   more
        disturbed   more beset

by some loss   such as
        he beside me whose shadow

looms over as he plays
        his music extra loud singing

extra louder to show how little
        he is afraid   of something still

scented but unseen   brown
        bear around the forest bend to whom the thought

of you has not occurred and so
        you shout its name in pretended gladness

Bear
Bear
Bear

Bear
Bear
Bear
Bear   before

the surprise of your aliveness can sharpen
its teeth.

ABOUT SUFFERING

for C. M.

Hard to know now where they stand, the Old Masters,
having themselves been lately subdued, reduced

to pondering ornate crusts in corners where
those whose opinion is no longer wanted await. Artisans of

the art of nothing left to offer. What shape now shows
her narrow dying on the bed, blanket rusted over the shrunk

nothing-sticks of her legs, her voice a gnat's whisper, what hue
for the still startling hum inside her bones, what shadow

when she opens her mouth to sip the broth, teeth
still sharp as points and gleaming, yellow as breakfast,

its jots of cozy buttered beads, spilled like the childhood
jitters whose disastrous appeal dripped down

your leg, making squelchy puddle in your shoe. Now
you too have nothing left to offer, task yourself to live

as if material to the hostile world and its refusals, unmoor
your most delicate ship, its sails more febrile

than all the bruises your lips can render on
skin, bringing forth rosy pocks bright as the shock

of a stray parakeet you once found roaming, as if
a presence chartreuse as ribbon could ever be

coincident. Once despite much vaunted
kindness I killed a creature like that, choked it

with milk from a dropper I held as if I believed
my hands were spiritual pliers of abundance, fit

to prise open smallest jaws. You alone can face
your need, what you lack or have been given,

the pleasure of sun on bare shoulders—to take this as divine
sign must be error when the sun brooks no notice with

personal crime, guilt or rot, a song indifferently
trampled under grass, some knoll gone, blue star that reminds

I can't show you what I refuse to know and can't save what
I refuse to see. Or if you can't bear the close air

of the dogs' untidy corner, take the key and the oar, pull up
your hair under dim streetlights where a car stops once,

twice, every time you clamber in, always saying
a no as profound as silence. Speaking of gifts, love

need not be returned and often isn't. Or if you stay,
you need be brave as dust, wiping your hands

on every surface, swept swiftly up as the seeds
of the morning glory, so quick to spread and thriving

everywhere unwanted and nowhere praised. Days
may pass under faithful watching. Later

the quiet accounting, what we can do
together, what we can do apart.

AUTOBIOGRAPHY

I was born in the province of I
and X was my due. I   could not
have predicted this level of fame
in a million years or more could not
have seen it coming. I   am
after all barred from looking at I
in the eye, how could I   have
seen how cunning how wild how the bright
spoke of greed in the eye spoke of ever
worsening confusions, I   wanting
to be greater than I, innumerable
everywhere I, to remain central
to the proceedings despite
the center's ceaseless moving. Never
lost I, always to be found there I   will
be accounted for, I insist upon it.
Therein lies the cunning of
the I. Rich and powerful,
esteemed as I, I   divides
into just principalities. For whatsoever
dazzles so long so light, grandeur,
splendor, killing star of the
I, I can offer only the enmity
of affection but I   does not wish
to harm. Disperse the riches of the I
in every barren field, I hope
they might flower, I   hopes,
still lightly afloat toward
shores of penury and gold.

▪▪▪

Autobiography of no mind but the mind I
am of. Flex that thought
of belonging, but I   has forgotten
speech. I who dots the landscape,
patiently waiting. Now
which I is this, who stands
in the hall, scraping
muddy boots. I   am so far
from the task of disguising my want,
my desire so bare it casts
arcane light in the beautiful rooms
where we might have stayed together,
quietly speaking. I   lacks the talent
to be other than I, to put I last
as God is said to have required. I   alone
in the kitchen where the dishes
are piled, wanting not
to be jilted but to be of use, not to
want but to give, I   in the quarters
of the hired hand, I will not be outcast
but useful to the rude reckoning
that must be done. I   won't
stand in the way, I will not ask, not
that I   deserves to know
but because I am asking. I   forgives
in advance, I's most intimate
stance. I saw the harm you did,
I forgive you still. I   entered
the eye of God and administered
mercy. There's nothing left
to forgive. So said I   succeeding
his example.

▪▪▪

I   thought to forget
the body. Leave
the body behind, in a shorn
meadow, supine and stripped, clothed
only in callus. Unwanted
want pierced the shadow of body
and it too was attractive. What the body
was too stupid to know despite
its relentless boasting, its desire
not equaled by hand or tongue. Saddest
episode of I, when I   persists
in asking, beyond
the resolve of genital
and breast, lobe and lip. I
longing for you as you were
before, when I crowded
your field of vision. Before I
gone grey aslant in a bewilder for when
I was kept and fastened. How costive to
I to see you so far, so
still in the light, how your eyes
scour expanses but never to glance
in my dim corridor where the touch
of the eye is the brasier's touch.
Lapse of the unseen I, there where I
is most unexpected, at the open market,
under rain, buying peaches. What I
asks is too much to ask. I know
what I withheld caused an irreparable
rift. It was the body
put me up to it.

▪▪▪

I   tried everything the mind
could be deft to, could not
become other than I. When
every moment I am less holy
when I am not and no longer
I. To all the friends
who called and called and
got no answer, I   knows
I did wrong. But you asked
for so little that the asking
was insult. When the jealousy of I
was beyond reprieve. When I
did you harm I knew you best,
that is no apology. Injuring you
I knew you best, like your palm
on my face in darkness. Come
with me to the deep graze
of the little asylum, I
should not like to be alone. If I
could be rid of I, if I
could follow the advice of my elders,
be confident and strong, realistic,
grounded, pragmatic, and real, to do
unto others as if I were other,
if I   could live as another, one life
for I, this life and no other, I   regrets
the harm I woke to, startle
of the animal in the wild,
or what I slept calmly through,
in the dreamless sleep
that is the held breath
of indifference.

▪ ▪ ▪

I was there from the start. When
you entered the room where I was alone
but I was there from the start. In the
beginning I was there, let no one
contest it. I took a running start, went
as far, far gone, sky gone, as I could
to no longer have I in view
but I was there from the start
and could not escape my notice. I encountering
I in the kitchen, slicing
apples for the sauce, having
no other concern, can this be true, I saw
I in the stairwell and gave
an earful to I, not liking
my attitude. I was all for I
until a nasty turn made I think
otherwise and then I was no longer
on my side. I stopped worrying then,
about the I. Who even knew, where
I had been. I keeps this record
of no expectation. I strives
to annotate the record of survival. As for
my smallest harms, most
specific feelings, if
you will never forget what I
once said, I will make
not forgetting lasting.

COMMON FIELD

We each carry
an oceanic sadness within
that opens wide as a door
with no hinges, admitting
everything.

I could tell every
belittlement, it would take
too much time, be too
costive. I could never say enough
to account for the cost.

Not that I think my suffering
is more. But I know it most
intimately, I know
its every curled fern,
from delicate green underside
to the beckoning finger. You

who have harmed me, I know
you want only to be seen.

I see you as I see the bright moon,
its white penny outline in
the afternoon sky, as I see
the mountain range in the distance
tipped clear with improbable
snow. A form I recognize
and that makes me feel at home
even if I cannot name it
and nor can it name me.

SECOND LIFE

n. the bottommost layer or depths of sediment that produce the nutrients required for flourishing (thrift) in the uppermost or surface layer (also known as first life)

GRANDMOTHER

Born in the municipality

of Y in the city of X. In 19XX met

the son of a Y-worker

from the coastal city of Z, a student

studying XX at Y University, at that time

young, pale, close

cropped, very dark beard, nothing

resembling the daft cordial he'd later become

in the era in which he was known

as Grandfather

rolling up the crumpled sleeves

of the square grey tunic he preferred despite

his devotion to

tea and toast   World Series   Pittsburgh Steelers

he was at that time

young, rather jovial, roly-poly, nothing

resembling the severe blade of Grandfather you'd later know

whose presence loomed, never a pleasure, only to

endure, whose hand

might thrust quickly out

with a slap or a coin or

butterscotch candy, brittle

patriarch whose hands agile

and strong had no need

to use a ruler, he was

at that time soft,

formless, *why I felt safe*

couldn't tell where he ended

or where he began. Colossal

hush of a man as ocean then War

changed

him and everything. Before

his inconceivable past, his future

beyond imagination, when he was

young and radiant, hope's vessel

hurtling toward the lyric

vanishing present.

THRIFT

She walked alone across the fields on her way home from school, eating the powdered ball of cocoa from the US Army ration box that had been distributed to all the children at lunchtime. If she walked too slowly, she would be late arriving home, suspicions raised, a sibling sent back to find her, she would be caught *en flagrant délit* and punished for having eaten the cocoa up, instead of bringing it home to share with the others. If she walked too quickly, she would not have time to brush the traces of powdered sugar from her lips, where they stubbornly clung, as clearly visible as the first flakes of snow on the hardened brown earth. The sugar's sweet white pimpling would give her away, more than the moist smell of chocolate on her skin, more than the serene look on her face, a look she rarely had, the look of someone who was satisfied.

GRANDFATHER

During the War went into hiding. Disappeared. Didn't see him for years. Couldn't wait for him to come home, we did nothing but wait, *cannot wait* was our vocation. Waited by vocation then we waited no longer. Then the novel apprenticeship, in the as-if he were-not. *He is not* was our vocation, his *not returning* our career. The tools for this task were mortar and pestle, yearning fragile, bark of laughter, thin shrug shrubbery. Sling these tools about your diminished waist at the ready. Years pass. War not finished but anyway Truce. One day he appeared

disheveled and happy, large brown suitcase filled with money. Where had he gone, where had he been, what had he done, whose suitcase, whose money, whose children, unholster the hands, for slender strokes and hard slaps. Within months he'd spent it all. Gambling.

AND/OR

The photograph is black and white, four by six, framed in white. She wears a collared minidress, slightly flared at the bottom, in a cut typical of the era, printed with crisply undulating geometric shapes, whose palette is difficult to envision freed from their angular sobriety of shades of grey. Chartreuse and rose, coral and teal, big bright saturated slashes. Her hair very black and forms waves that frame a round, pretty face, caught in an expression of mild surprise. Not an unhappy surprise but without, strictly speaking, much evidence of happiness either.

▪ ▪ ▪

In the photograph she perches on a large, flat rock, barely lapped by a ripple of waves visible at the right edge of the frame. She appears to be leaning back on the rock for balance, but because she is lithe and long and the rock not very large, a small, bent awkwardness interrupts her pose, so that she appears not as if balancing gracefully on outstretched arms but rather as if pressing down uncomfortably, a palpable sense of cramping discomfort intruding into the stillness of the seaside photograph, the feeling of an object on the verge of collapse.

▪▪▪

The photograph is overexposed and the mother's face gleams unnaturally white. A young woman, with short, dark wavy hair, surrounded by four boys. The boys surround her in such a way that only her face and the neckline of the patterned collar of her dress or coat can be seen. The youngest boy sits on her knee, a chubby toddler wrinkling his brow or, perhaps, squinting at the sun. Possibly a sunny day. Unlike his brothers, who are each laced up in a dark school uniform each adorned with a row of six large white buttons, the youngest wears a white pinafore and blouse, whose sleeves are clearly too long, given their thick bunched folds at his wrists. The boys' hair is shorn tightly against their skulls, a row of dark fingernails clipped too short. Neither the boys nor their mother smile, nor do they frown. They look unwaveringly at the camera, with five mouths set in identically ambiguous lines. No father is present. He is absent and/or dead.

▪▪▪

The slash gashes, pinky finger dipped in ink. And pierces. Absent and/or dead Father who is also Grandfather, although dead Father becomes Grandfather only by inference. Syntactical Grandfather. This too makes a kind of piercing. Absent and/or dead Father who might have been Grandfather in the still distant future but who died before he could fulfill his truncated destiny of Grandchildren, riddle: what kind of Grandfather has no Grandchildren? An absent and/or dead Father whose body inhabits the corpse who reduces us to reading signs of absence, sense, and presence.

White poppies bloom duskly in the nightfield.

WE WILL NOT SURVIVE THIS HAVING A BODY

every morning balsam stains
red our nails wrapped

in crushed petals held
close by string and leaves

of the bush flowering behind
the plaster walling

the room where I and
they sleep having never

not slept where anyone
could enter any

time having never not
shared a cloth

to wash my face having
never taken space

in a bed not
borrowed

WHAT YOU CAN'T DO WITHOUT

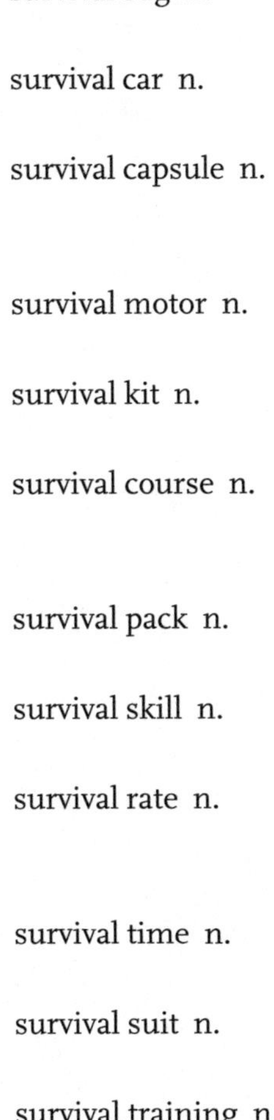

survival bag n.

survival car n.

survival capsule n.

survival motor n.

survival kit n.

survival course n.

survival pack n.

survival skill n.

survival rate n.

survival time n.

survival suit n.

survival training n.

survival curve n.

survival use n.

survival horror n.

WHAT WAS SAID

She was *a hot-tempered disagreeable young woman.*
She was

forbidden to study. She ran away
to Japan,

to pursue her studies in X. She was *rebellious*
and visionary. Smallest

in the photograph, row of soberly smiling
young girls in kimonos. Later

supine in a hospital bed, leg amputated, glance averted.
She

lost her leg to diabetes and
grief. She died

over Eldest Uncle. You don't know me, the first and last
you saw of her.

She was strewn across the bed *I miss*
my mother. Mother

has herself a mother did that mother

too have a mother
vertiginous array of

mothers subsumed into mirrors
unaccountable not

countable repetitions of mothers, which
language can count

every mother, mother's
language,

the language of the child
without mother, the language

of the child become
mother or

motherless, the child
who lost her mother's

tongue.

FIRST MATERNAL UNCLE

Colon cancer, Second Uncle. No, First Uncle, paternal side. No, the former colon, the latter emphysema. The latter a businessman, failed. No, he was rich, he traded in furs. The former a dandy. On his deathbed asked for Chanel cologne. When he was young, he resembled Alain Delon.

Went to vet school, paid for by his sisters. No, a hygienist, dental school. Later taught English to the grannies down the block. He taught the ladies very well. Cried to his wife in the days before he died. *Forgive me, I have been with a prostitute.* Grannies practiced taking *busse* back to the *apateu*. Not faithful. Pious. Prayed daily but got no relief. One had two sons, who now live with their mother. No, no sons, only daughters, who played the piano very well. Though the middle girl was met with contempt. The mother tongue says: you will kill me, it's unbearable, my worry's a mountain, you're an idiot, you have no brain, I'll die of it, I despise you. The words slip wetly out the mouths of elders with the indifference of electric eels. Only in the ears of the children do they produce their special uncanny effect, through which they compete with the inexorable immutability of the actual.

MYSTERIOUS DISTRESS

Uncle's cancer,
Auntie's stroke,
Grandfather's stomach
ailment. Grandmother,
diabetic? Anyway, leg
amputated (*when*). Maternal
Grandfather, old age. Sixty. Cancer,
suitcase word for secret. Secret
smoking, always, stress. Cancer,
stomach, heartache, stomach
problem, stroke problem, ache,
affliction, seizure, suicide, he
felt a sudden ache, cancer of
the stomach, the anus, the blood,
somewhere (*a sudden ache*), perhaps
a lung. He felt an ache and
his corpse followed
its pierced directive. She lost
her leg (*you were busy*
with school) she died
of grief, she couldn't get
out of bed. Laid in
bed for over four years. (*The summer*
we drove to Florida.)

▪▪▪

History of blindness, cancer, diabetes, heart disease, stroke

dementia, hypertension, insanity, depression

allergies to medication or anesthesia

high cholesterol, blood pressure, drug addiction, alcoholism

preeclampsia, rage, postpartum depression

pedophilia, permissiveness, musical talent, high

IQ, low IQ, culinary skill, short temper, cleft palate

acuity, willfulness, criminality, shame, onanism, bed-

wetting, excessive laughter, artistic merit, ambidexterity

shyness, suicidal ideation, risk of self-harm

maybe, certainly, possibly, likely, unlikely, doubtful

sans doute they existed

having passed through the world without admission.

▪ ▪ ▪

If you exist I will never see the field at night but must
see you keeping meter, marking soft abject landing, your hand

not touching me not there, its not-thereness existence. Seeing
you in the field I see the field you dreamt you looked into

at night where you could see yourself standing, field without
anger, no more real than a dream, you dreamt you looked

into the field at night and could see the secret unravel. Before
you can see, you must be seen, surrounded from a distance,

followed about, penetrated through, held in strange power as
if being seen might transform into forms of seeing. As

if your future body, whose lungs' prudence, limbs' binding,
heart's thick viscous pump you will not survive, yet

when you look, you look without anger, you love the world,
what exists in the world, the world of the field, the field

of the bounded world.

▪ ▪ ▪

Then one fall evening his father
fell to the floor. Never
got back up. Little Uncle
five. Big Uncle twelve and Second Uncle ten,
sent to fetch the doctor. Too
late. The day before he'd complained
of a stomachache. That may well be
but no one dies
of a stomachache. His heart
stopping maybe or somewhere
a cancer. The day before your father
had a dream. He saw
an airplane and his father
dressed for travel. In the dream
his father waved goodbye and
that was it. Just the day
before. He was nine,
second youngest. Remarry,
a widow with four sons? No
not possible. Anyway not
the way she chose. She chose
seminary. You see why
he doesn't know
how to be a father.
It isn't that he isn't
trying. He's trying
but he doesn't know how.

FAILURE TO THRIVE

You are still too young to have any secrets. We are still too young to have real secrets. At your age, only family secrets. At our age, familial secrets. He coerced her, got her pregnant. She was sent back to her village, who knows what became of her. You slept with him once but it took. Stumbling upstairs, tripped and fell, in a flash you knew. He cheated on the exam and won first place. But a boy saw and lorded it over him, all those years. You cheated on the test and got second prize. She got an abortion in a small city on the coast. You paid in cash, a wad of waitressing tips. She worked in the bank basement, counting money. Dozens of girls, counting piles of bills. Every day her white gloves the color of soot. You temped in a bank, you watched your boss. He lived in the suburbs, with a wife and three children. You wrote his home address on a Post-it, which you carried in your cardigan pocket. One day she wrote in her diary "He's back" and that was all. That night, the tables and chairs all overturned.

▪ ▪ ▪

War began but ended and/or didn't end, Truce was called, Occupation began until it ended, they arrived, the Japanese withdrew, the Japanese arrived, she was born, he disappeared, the Americans came, he was born, he came back, she died, she was fired, she got pregnant, she would have been there, he would have lived there then, would she have known, would she have been old enough, wouldn't she have moved, wouldn't she have not yet been born, wouldn't the war have ended, wouldn't War have kept them home, kept them moving, what money? How could she have been there, at that time, in the city of X, in the house of Y, caring for XX, who had died in XY in 19XX, how could she have known, how could he not have guessed it?

▪▪▪

Auntie visits from the home country. Hello
goodbye how are you nice to see you
steal a crust, a bribe, a bit, a scrap
of parchment paper. Face heretofore
seen in representation. You could put your hand
through that taut skin, as it opens
its empty sleeve to receive you. She brings
a gift of an enameled jewelry box, in exchange
for your gift of nothing. *Discourteous*
to strangers who arrive
at your village, you will soon find
you are everywhere a stranger.

▪ ▪ ▪

When I was a child, she'd call me loudly to
the shower to scrub her back with a rough
red glove. Sloughing off the dried skin and
dirt called *black noodles*. Her hands beautiful,
braced against tile, fingers already subtly
hooked as rakes in parched fields. I have
the same hands now. When a bad thing
happens, she goes over it over and again,
transforming a note that can't be swallowed
into janky song, squeezed through a cracked
and broken reed. I picture her body as landscape,
a broad meadow dotted with stalks of stubborn
green. You will have picked a bouquet of burst,
weedy flowers not knowing they're the blinking
lights of small neglected engines. Friends say
my mother is beautiful, chic, elegant, and
sweet. I have stood in the kitchen rigid
with anger and made my mother weep.

LAST GEM GLITTERS BRIGHTLY

Little sister of the last year of Occupation, only child
to keep her name: *the last gem*, a wish, desire,

a warding-off: let there be no more. But another came,
a boy, a dandy, whetted and fine as a blade, dangling

cigarettes from long tapered fingers, the girls coyly
calling *Hey hey Alain Delon!* From his father only

scorn for these virile insufficiencies. Father
himself whose every endeavor ended

in failure, who broke every thing he touched, fired
many times, unemployed many years, wasted bagfuls

of cash. Many women loved him, only
not his wife. He wrote his daughter in America for

Chanel aftershave. She tried over and again to address
thc package, but resentment crooked

her fingers so the characters collapsed. Later, he
died. His ashes somewhere scattered. Somewhere

in the town of X, he produced a son, who bore
not his name but the name of his mother. Now mother's

rituals of martyrdom commingle anorexia and senior
citizenry in an endless and irritating flow of

breakfast that flows into snack that flows into lunch that flows
into snack that flows into limitless dinner followed

by fruit, snacks, more snacks. But she eats nothing,
hovers over and around, refusing to sit, taking one bite

then jumping up to open the fridge behind
her chair, taking one bite then jumping up to stir

the soup that will be eaten tomorrow, while her granddaughter
stuffs square after square after square of gim into her mouth, pulling

each from the small foil-covered plastic tray that probably can't be
recycled. Mother was not the youngest but the youngest was

a boy and his maleness countermanded his bottom-rank, while mother
was only next-to-youngest but a girl, therefore her bottom-rank status

multiply enforced. The drumstick that went to her never, or if she ever
reached for a single square of gim—*do you plan to eat a piece with*

every bite?— now she picks up the choicest pieces, scatters
them like jewels, everywhere but on her plate.

THE REALITY EFFECT

In the era before he abandoned the First Wife by finally taking his affairs and moving far away to the province of XX where nobody would bother to look for him, every Chuseok he and First Wife used to throw a Disguise Party, where every guest was required to wear a disguise that invoked the harvest, although all were always outdone by First Wife, who might cleverly hide behind filigreed masks woven from stalks of barley, or drape herself suavely in panels of silk dyed blushed peach as the tips of new chrysanthemum. This was one of First Wife's many talents that were bitterly mourned when she was discarded in favor of Second Wife, who in turn complained bitterly that First Wife's subsequent threats to kill herself were an obnoxious form of vindictive hysteria aimed solely at upending her status as new Wife. We didn't like Second Wife, for this and other cruelties, but over time, because Second Wife was part of reality, and First Wife no longer real but merely a mirage of the past, even if we could not entirely subdue our dislike, we were obliged to transform it into tolerable form, some form that could sustain our parallel living, if we wanted to live in reality, the real that is inhabited only by survivors.

NOTES

The epigraph to "Death of the Mother" cites an apocryphal telegram that Greta Garbo is alleged to have sent to her agent, according to biographer Robert Gottlieb.

"Cat Love" reimagines the anecdote "The Hermit with the Cat" from *The Golden Legend,* Jacobus de Voragine's 1260 compilation of the lives of the saints, to which Roland Barthes alludes in a lecture on animals during the January 26 session of his 1977 Collège de France seminar, "Comment vivre ensemble" ("How to live together").

The title "I Like I Don't Like" loosely translates the title of an entry in Barthes's autobiographical *Roland Barthes par Roland Barthes.* "The You You Do or Don't Resemble" loosely translates a photo caption found in *Roland Barthes par Roland Barthes.*

The epigraph to "As If" loosely translates from *La préparation du roman* (*The preparation of the novel*), the published transcription of one of Barthes's seminars.

"Mysterious Distress" borrows from Donald Winnicott's idea that for the infant, being seen is the prerequisite to being able to see, and from an account in Pierre-Armand Dufau's 1876 book *Souvenirs et impressions d'une jeune aveugle-née* of a 12-year-old blind girl's understanding of what it means to be seen without being able to see: "Whereas I could make contact with [other people] by touch and hearing, they were bound to me through an unknown sense, which entirely surrounded me even from a distance, followed me about, penetrated through me and somehow held me in its power from morning to night" (translated by Peter Heath in Marius von Senden's *Space and Sight,* first published in 1932 as *Raum-und Gestaltauffassung bei operierten Blindgeborenen*).

ACKNOWLEDGMENTS

Gratitude to the editors who published earlier versions of poems in the following journals: *Action, Spectacle*; *Oversound*; *Provincetown Arts*; *The Spectacle*; *The Volta*.

Many thanks to the patient and perspicacious team at the University of Iowa Press, especially Meghan Anderson, Elizabeth Sheridan-Drake, Lily Giddings, and Susan Hill Newton.

I would not have been able to write this book without material assistance from many. I am deeply thankful to Don Mee Choi, Duriel Harris, Anna Maria Hong, Mona Jazayeri, Juliet Jacobson, Caitie Moore, Saretta Morgan, Susie Pourfar, Prageeta Sharma, Andrew Smith, Jennifer Sweeney, and Christopher van Ginhoven Rey for giving me space and time, invitations, art, hospitality, jobs, critique, and other forms of support that helped me renew, day after day, the conditions for the possibility of writing.

Profound gratitude to Lisa Wells and Joshua Marie Wilkinson. Thank you to Brandon Shimoda for his anchoring friendship.

Gratitude to my family—past and present, future and imagined, phantoms and ancestors.

To Munro, who remained through deepest night.

This book is for Musa.

KUHL HOUSE POETS

Christopher Bolin
Anthem Speed

Christopher Bolin
Ascension Theory

Christopher Bolin
Form from Form

Shane Book
All Black Everything

Shane Book
Congotronic

Oni Buchanan
Must a Violence

Oni Buchanan
Time Being

Michele Glazer
fretwork

Michele Glazer
On Tact, & the Made Up World

David Micah Greenberg
Planned Solstice

Jeff Griffin
Lost and

Hajar Hussaini
Disbound

John Isles
Ark

John Isles
Inverse Sky

Youna Kwak
For This and Other Cruelties

Jessica Laser
The Goner School

Aaron McCollough
Rank

Aaron McCollough
Salms

Randall Potts
Trickster

Bin Ramke
Airs, Waters, Places

Bin Ramke
Matter

Michelle Robinson
The Life of a Hunter

Vanessa Roveto
bodys

Vanessa Roveto
a women

Robyn Schiff
Revolver

Robyn Schiff
Worth

Sarah V. Schweig
Take Nothing with You

Rod Smith
Deed

Donna Stonecipher
Transaction Histories

Cole Swensen
The Book of a Hundred Hands

Cole Swensen
Such Rich Hour

Tony Tost
Complex Sleep

Pimone Triplett
Supply Chain

Nick Twemlow
Attributed to the Harrow Painter

Susan Wheeler
Meme

Emily Wilson
The Keep